Mappings

By the same author

FICTION

The Golden Gate: A Novel in Verse

A Suitable Boy

An Equal Music

POETRY

The Humble Administrator's Garden

All You Who Sleep Tonight

Three Chinese Poets (translations)

Beastly Tales from Here and There (fables)

Arion and the Dolphin (libretto)

The Rivered Earth (libretti)

Summer Requiem

NON-FICTION

Two Lives

From Heaven Lake: Travels through Sinkiang and Tibet

Mappings

VIKRAM SETH

SPEAKING
TIGER

SPEAKING TIGER BOOKS LLP
125A, Ground floor, Shahpur Jat, near Asiad Village
New Delhi – 110049

First published by Writers Workshop, 1981
Revised edition first published by Penguin Books India, 1994
This edition published by Speaking Tiger Books 2021

Some of the poems in this collection were first published by
The Threepenny Review, *London Magazine*, Seqoia Press and *Blue Unicorn*.

ISBN: 978-93-5447-103-2

10 9 8 7 6 5 4 3 2 1

For sale in the Indian Subcontinent only

Typeset in AldineBT by SÜRYA, New Delhi
Printed at Chaman Enterprises, New Delhi

For
Tim Steele
&
Donald Davie

Contents

Introduction to the 1994 Edition 9

Panipat 13
Sea and Desert 15
A Winter Word 16
Departure Lounge 17
Quaking Bridge 23
Switching Off 24
Sonnet 25
Grand Canyon 26
To a Fellow-Traveller 27
Rakhi 30
Tomatoes 32
Home Thoughts from the Bay 33
Rain 34
From the Memoirs of Babur,
First Moghul Emperor of Hindustan 35
To Manijeh 37
The Walkers 39
Time-Zones 40
After Three Years 41
From Mount Tamalpais 42
Thoughts While Travelling at Night 43
Aubade 44

The Yellow Cricket 45
The Sultan's Turret 46
At Evening 47
Moonless Night 48
Guest 49
The Balcony 50
Even Such 51
Close of Play 52
Last Night 55
Party for the Retirement of the Oldest-Serving British Museum Reading Room Book Attendant 56
Dubious 57
Bagatelles 58
The Tale of Melon City 60
Six Octets 65
Distressful Homonyms 68
Progress Report 69
Point Reyes 70
Sleep and Death 71
Mappings 72
Moths 74
Divali 75
A Morning Walk 81
Stump 84

Introduction to the 1994 Edition

I wrote the poems that appear in this book in my twenties, when I was a student in England and, later, California. Since I was studying Economics, not English, I stood outside the orbit of the latest critical theories, and did not realize that writing in rhyme and metre would make me a sort of literary untouchable. In due course, I sent my manuscript to almost every publisher I had heard of. After innumerable, increasingly painful rejections, I decided to typeset and publish it myself. I dedicated it to the two English teachers at Stanford who had gone out of their way to encourage, inspire, and (not least of all) criticize my efforts.

When the slim, stapled, paperbound volume of *Mappings* with its black and white cover came off the press in 1980, I proudly peddled it around various bookstores in the San Francisco Bay area. Not many, however, were willing to stock, let alone buy, the first fruits of my self-determined genius. I then forced copies on my friends and family, telling them to sell them if they could, and to give them away if they couldn't. Meanwhile, I went off to China for two years of travel and economic research. Although I had printed an address in the book for the benefit of enthusiastic readers who wished to re-order copies, I don't believe that anyone used it.

After a year in China, I returned home to Delhi for a visit. On a short trip to Calcutta I met Professor P. Lal, and he published *Mappings* in 1981 in an elegant orange sari-clad version under the imprint of the Writers Workshop. He was thus my first publisher—and I, like many other Indian writers in English, owe him a debt of esteem and gratitude.

Ten years passed, and other matters took over my time and mind. Occasionally someone would tell me that they had read a copy of *Mappings* in a library or at the home of a friend. The book had gone out of print, and I had no thought of resuscitating it. Then I discovered that a second edition had been brought out by Writers Workshop in 1991, this time, unfortunately, peppered with misprints.

When Penguin India asked me for permission to republish *Mappings*, I hesitated. On the one hand, I was keen that the work should appear in an accurate version if it had to appear at all. On the other, I wondered about the poems themselves, some of which now struck me as embarrassingly callow. I did not wish to make my readers cringe by offering them a second helping of my juvenilia. But a friend (whose opinions are always forthright if sometimes eccentric) told me that she much preferred my voice in *Mappings* to that of my later books of poems. Whether I agreed with that slightly alarming judgement or not, I felt that I ought not to withdraw a book that had elicited it.

I have, however, made a few amendments: I have excised two footnotes; removed the originals (more picturesque than helpful) of the four translated poems; and in two poems changed a word or phrase. In 'Guest', 'entirely' has been replaced by 'utterly'. In 'Moonless Night', the phrase 'the reciprocal certainty' has been altered, and as a result the meaning of the line is now very different from what it was before. I am not sure that all this is justifiable. Readers get attached to particular incarnations of a work, and I myself have become quite indignant when I have read an updated, 'authoritative' version of a well-loved poem. Perhaps the authority of authors should lapse with their first editions, and they should be forbidden from tampering with their own published work in the name of improvement. My excuse (for what it is worth) is that in both cases I have in fact restored the wording of an earlier draft which I had revised in what now seems to me a mistaken attempt at polish.

Delhi
February 1994

VIKRAM SETH

Panipat

My aunts sit in the courtyard,
Gossiping, shelling peas,
While around them parrots
Cackle in the neem trees.

I sit with my flute near the place
Where the well was covered up
To make a septic tank.
I glide from stop to stop

Following the scale of Lalit
Though it is afternoon;
Its mournful meditative
Mood moves into a tune

Leading me God knows where—
Into a universe
Beyond—beyond Panipat!
Well, I could have done worse ~*

* a stanza break at the end of a page is marked by ~
and no stanza break at the end of a page is marked by ≁

Than break my studies and come
Back home from Inglistan.
Punjab, pandits, panir,
Panipat and pān,

Family, music, faces,
Food, land, everything
Drew me back, yet now
To hear the koyal sing

Brings notes of other birds,
The nightingale, the wren,
The blackbird; and my heart's
Barometer turns down.

I think of beeches, elms,
And stare at the neem tree.
My cousin slices a mango
And offers it to me.

I choose the slice with the seed
And learn from the sweet taste,
Well-known and alien,
I must be home at last.

Sea and Desert

How do I merit such happiness? To have
The moon, the Pacific, and you beside me, waking
At three to sudden cold—dew, the stiff breeze
Along the headland; I have been watching you,
Your face lit in the full moon, restless, still,
As out beyond the strip of foam near the crags
Below, the moon lights up a calm yet shifting
Track on the ocean. Your face with its
Clean lines and tousled hair is beautiful
And it is hard to believe that even in
This stark and lovely place it is the cause
Of so much of my peace. You sleep again,
And I know this unusual beauty, that you've
Neither aimed for nor deserved, will recur
Again and again for me with sea and moon,
An image changing with these changing things,
Distracting me from neither, enhancing both,
A gift you could not help but give, something
I too have neither aimed for nor deserve.

A Winter Word

Cold cold friend, Frost—
Night comes, and I
Am dispossessed.
Most cold, cold
Is this night;
And my youth old,
My spirit lost.
I cannot rest.
I walk alone.
Frost, burn upon
My every bone.

Departure Lounge

Among the lobsters and pushcarts
At Boston Airport we
Walk up and down, father and son
Knowing that we will be
Apart for years now, talking and regretting
The shortness of this meeting.

Four days of a New England Spring;
I recall one Monsoon
—Calcutta—when one night I gave
A 50-paise coin
To a girl in rags. You had forbidden it
And I cannot forget

The nature of your punishment.
It was not words or blows.
I had had beatings; as for words,
There were not many of those,
Sharp, or warm, between us. What you said
Was that you'd cut me dead.

~

I had ignored your stated will
And would be ignored
From that day on: the status quo
No doubt; but when I heard
You say the express words, it was to me
Unneeded cruelty.

I had few memories of your love
Or kindness, even speech.
'The chapatis are well-cooked'; 'Stop that
At once.' How could you reach
To me through those? How could I understand
What lay behind your hand?

My act to you had one intent,
To thwart you. I recall
The fear, hate, the contempt I felt
At that. It would appal
That sixteen-year-old to observe in me
The opposite of all three.

But what has changed, Papa? Those years
I'd have wished different
Are lost. Is it that fatherhood,
Perhaps now imminent,
Reframes my views of what a father means?
Or that those clear-edged scenes

Of boyhood are less focused now;
Since I no longer hate
'The self they made me' I can free

The myths that bore the freight
Of self-dislike, self-pity and despair?
Or is it that we are

In noncontiguous domains
And can afford our smiles,
Non-grating greetings and exchange
Over the frictionless miles?
All? None of the above? Whatever's true
I know that I love you

Far less for these than that I see
What I could not then know
—You doubtless thought it manifest—
Your love for us. Although
You gave us food and comforts, were obsessed
With 'Nothing but the best

Will do for *my* kids,' it was time,
The costless priceless salt
We lacked, that you spared only to
Dislodge some leechlike fault.
I never grew inured to the blurred fear
I sensed when you were near.

You screened your griefs; you sheltered us.
For one who in his youth
Is both a part of and apart
From those he loves, the truth
Of what he feels, if difficult to bear
Is harder yet to share.

~

Orphaned at two, you ran away
From Baoji at fifteen.
The tin shack, the Mussourie store,
Hunger, the freezing rain,
Nothing could split the shell of hurt and pride.
You would have rather died

Than faced that uneasy ease again.
Unsure of tenderness
Where you most craved it, did it grow
Too anguished to express?
You screened your love; though Mama says you cried
The day Baoji died.

Well, I was blind; but it was dark
And both of us have moved
Into a clearer sunlight. I, now
Certain that I was loved,
See you, too, mellowed. Age? Doubtless. But more;
The carapace you wore

Could have withstood that. Something's given
In your philosophy.
'Relaxing' then was one more stern
Programmed activity.
Yet today to walk a Boston square
Savouring what we share—

Threads of light rain, the reflected church,
Talk of the family;
Your work and mine; your paradigm

For paradise—greenery
And a small river; Delhi politics;
Aradhana's latest tricks—

Brings you a peace that draws me inwards;
And the unrigid heart
With which you view my views, my loves,
However far apart
From yours, seasons the warmth I newly sense
With a vivid tolerance

Of living day to day. You could,
I know, live mile to mile.
Long distance runners learn to bear
Segmented pain. But while
The college marathon and the torturous
Disease you've borne taught this,

They did not teach its partner-art,
To live with happiness
In what is an unfinished state
Till we die. You possess
What was not there then when I was a boy,
This uninvasive joy.

Yet somewhat late for me, I think.
I have moved on, my life
Twelve thousand miles from yours, my ways
Safe from paternal strife,
Paternal judgement and—how can I tell—
Paternal love as well?

Your arm around my shoulder, we
Stroll through the lounge. The hand
Arcs round the clock; flight 43
Is called; I understand
The weight of fatherhood can survive the day
That a child moves away.

We meet on neutral ground: next time
May be at home. I should
Tell you as you walk through the door
I'll miss you. If I could
Have had a better father years ago
I could not now, I know.

Quaking Bridge

So here I am again by Quaking Bridge,
Standing a moment by the water's edge,
Hearing the water's roar as it churns past
The ancient brewery; and I am cast
Back to December when by Quaking Bridge
I stood a moment by the water's edge
And heard the water's turbulence, and knew
That since no more remained that I could do
And since to think of pain itself is pain,
I should forget and not walk here again
And hear the water under Quaking Bridge
And stand in thought beside the water's edge,
And I am here again; but why delay?
Think, and walk on, and think: but walk away.

Switching Off

There are no fears of undiscovered countries
Or bournes from which no traveller returns
To one who knows this life is all there is;
So when he feels it has become oppressive,
The effort of drawing breath exhausts and strains him
And dispriz'd love, and whips and scorns etcetera
Have mangled him, why does he not switch off?

Perhaps the thought that, having once been happy
(And stirred by the analogy of life
Being a wheel) he will again be so;
Or some imagined, as yet unseen sight,
Like Halley's Comet lighting up the sky
For which he'd have to wait till '86;
Or else objective curiosity:
Who will be President in ten years' time?
Who'll win the hockey in the Olympic Games?
And then his family: although he knows
When dead there's no remorse, he cannot bear
That they, remaining, feel he did not love them—
It is such things that hold him to the earth
And not the dread of something after death.

Sonnet

O my generous and exuberant love
As the slow moon coldly slopes down the sky
The pines hum to themselves and you to yourself
And you pass your hands across my face.
My hands stray—stray?—to your breasts,
Small, such as angels probably are permitted.
You are forgiven, solely because of them
For beating me at Scrabble.

Dear friend you cannot know
How much you fill my days—and the long nights,
When outside the whole world is threatening silence,
The pine is swaying in a senseless dream,
Your hand within my hand, your warm warm body
Close by me, and in the dark your unseen smile.

Grand Canyon

Swift dawn across the falling wall below;
The billion-year-old schist—and the powdered snow
Of yesterday caught in the juniper limb
Leaning wind-warped over the sheer South Rim.

To a Fellow-Traveller

Dear Madeleine, I dip my Pepperidge Farm
Cookie into my tea and think of you
And how you laughed and held me by the arm

On Shattuck when I left. Though I'm one who
Believes that between strangers there should be
A proper distance kept—between us two

Who have not sipped each other's company
For even a day, I'd happily dispense
With distance, logic or consistency.

I love you! Let us meet again. I sense
This may be read and smiled at and rejected
As overripe Parnassian pretence;

The honesty of prose is less suspected—
This is not Florence in 1293
When rhyme was reasonable, but I've elected

To do it this way both because for me
It's fun, and—yes—to re-elicit that smile
It set my spirit yodelling to see. ~

At Newark Airport, brooding all the while
On DC10s and engine failure
I thought I saw a sign above the aisle,

'All hope abandon, ye who enter here.
The pilot is obtuse, the plane is late,
The flight attendants flighty, and the sheer

Monotony of a sedentary state
Maintained for seven hours will likely drive
You into lunacy, or at any rate

To morbid introspection. You'll arrive
At Oakland, high-strung and (in spirits) low,
Lost in your past, scared by the future.' I've

Known many flights like this. How could I know
That what I would recall about this flight
Would not be doom and polythene, but the snow-

Fluffed cloud-terrain heavy with evening light,
Your laughter, Dante, and the darkening flare
Of the chased sunset merging with the night?

I'd always hoped somehow, sometime, somewhere
I'd meet someone like you. I also deemed
Such visions built on vodka and on air.

And so this was, and yet to me it seemed
Even when we stood on sober earth again
That neither of us wished it had been dreamed. ~

So what do you say? I don't care where or when.
I have your number but am somewhat chary
Of using it. Will you call me? And then

The two of us could meet. You know I'm wary
Of ruffling the calm waters of your mind,
But mine are ruffled. I sip a Bloody Mary

Or dunk a pseudo-madeleine and find
Your face before me—as when two hours ago
I browsed through 'Heaven'; and when such things remind

Me of your voice, the short shard of rainbow
Above the clouds, the layered sky above—
'Chartreuse, turquoise, red sherbet, indigo . . .'

(Remember?)—I remember you with love
Richer than I believed seven swift hours
Could ever wake; perhaps some semblance of

The love that moves the sun and the other stars.

Rakhi
for Aradhana

I had forgotten the time
Of year. Your rakhi came,
Showing how things have changed
And are the same.

It was a contract of trust
With more than you. I know
I left home too many
Years ago.

I place the golden thread
Across my wrist; that done,
Struggle with my left hand
To tie it on.

You should have done that; I
Too have lost half the rite.
I promise you your gift
In '78.

Those future numerals
Look curious; and your brother
Too will be strange when next
We meet each other.

How we must both have changed;
Only the custom stays,
Educing from the past
The undying days.

Tomatoes

The slugs have got to the tomatoes.
The corn is dead. The wooden poles no longer
Hold up the chicken wire. Gopher's
Burrows cover the spot where I stood
And watched the sun sink below the tendrils
Still articulate with spray. Mint
And the nameless blueflowered weed
Have covered it all—quiet and quick;
One plot of a hundred similar ones,
Odd child of lazy parents.

Not now too lovesome a thing, God wot.
Nothing to mark the labour of hoeing the ground—
Bread and cheese and beer in the thorn-tree's shade, the sweat
And laughter. Marvelling at the
Bloated zucchini of the neighbouring plot;
A swim in the lake afterwards. The land
Is patient but not infinitely so.
After you went it became an effort to water,
Weed, mulch, replant, even harvest the rich
Recurring crop. I went to the Co-op instead.
Oh well,
Those tomatoes were far too expensive anyway:
My bike was punctured twice by nearby thorns.

Home Thoughts from the Bay

Down Highway 101 the van
Hurtles with all the speed it can
And all the passengers but one
Have jolted off to sleep. The sun
Strikes long apocalyptic lines
Of corrugated sheds, the tines
Of Sutro Tower, billboards, wires,
The airport, scrap, discarded tyres;
And I who must commute each day
Along the grimy-margined Bay
Dizzied by each high-octane breath
And tired of work and bored to death
And sick for home decide I ought
To check that surrogate for thought,
The Highway I-Ching—which today
States 'Yield.' 'Keep Right.' 'Go Back. Wrong Way.'
Should I fly home? Why am I here?
And yield to what? To whim? Fate? Fear?
Keep Right . . . My eyes obey and there
Pursue a jumbo-jet to where
This afternoon high in the sky
A half moon loiters absently by,
Incognizant of why or what
Or where it ought to be or not.

Rain

The rain drips quietly down
    The windowpane
Through nightfall, midnight, on
    To sublit dawn.

The sleeping bag is warm,
    The little room
Suffices for a time
    For world, for home.

May too much light not fall
    Across the sill
Onto the rug, the wall.
    For this slow while

May the cool pattering souse
    The unquenched trees
And these assuaging greys
    Rest on my eyes.

From the Memoirs of Babur, First Moghul Emperor of Hindustan

The snows near Chiraghdan
Covered the roads. Our guide,
Like us, was lost. We sent
Out men to find the road.
And still it snowed and snowed.

Four days passed: they returned.
They had not found a soul.
No sign of settlement,
No wandering tribesmen; hill
On hill, and that was all.

We knew we must advance
Into the breast-deep snow.
As the first man lost strength
He was replaced. I, too,
Helped press it down. This way

In a week we pushed ourselves
Three miles, or perhaps less.
Regardless of their rank,
Though I left them the choice,
Few men remained on horse.

We halted by a cave.
That evening the wind blew
So sharply through the fierce
And fearsome drifts of snow
We all expected to die.

I dug a prayer-mat's space
Close to the mouth with a hoe
And knelt. The cave seemed small.
Though some desired that I
Go in, I did not go.

When almost at midnight
A survey party discovered
The cave could hold us all
I shook the snow from my head
And entered. Such as had food

—Preserved flesh or stewed meat—
Produced it. Thus we moved
From the inhuman cold
Into the warmth of the cave
Where all at length were safe.

To Manijeh

O Scorpio-cat
When you have gone
My eyes will turn
To lumps of stone.

I'll look at ice
And think of how
You called it 'bairf'.
I'll eat pilao

And taste your touch
Where it won't be.
How will I bear
To read Rumi?

Raga Darbari,
The taste of dill
And all clean mirrors
Will make me ill.

Windex will lie
Where it was laid,
The record player
Sit unplayed,

~

And dill may grow
Ten feet in height
But will no longer
Yield delight.

At reference to
Shirazi Turks
My stricken heart
Will beat in jerks—

But worst, some random
Woman's clear laugh
Will neatly cut
My liver in half.

The Walkers

They walked towards a trigonometrical point
along a ridge; as they approached, a brace
of startled ravens suddenly rose in joint
defensive chorus for their living-space.

The walkers laughed companionably; then one
who filled the other's heart with clear delight
said, pointing up at Snowdon, 'Look, the sun
has not yet thawed the snow; no, there, that white—'

The other looked; the abrasive poignancy
of the ravens' cries, their dark extended wings
spoke of no parting, and he did not see
the decay inherent in contingent things.

Time-Zones

I willed my love to dream of me last night
    That we might lie
At peace, if not beneath a single sheet,
    Under one sky.

I dreamed of her but she could not alas
    Humour my will;
It struck me suddenly that where she was
    Was daylight still.

After Three Years

Charred grass (the drought); the birch stump (last year's
gales);
Discoloured rose-leaves. Yet at the lawn's cropped edge
Orange azaleas flame; beyond the hedge
The sunset reddens steeply towards North Wales.

Blight; change, recurrence—I am at it again.
Your illness; meaning; the old neurotic search.
Instead of the woodpecker on the birch
A crazy jackdaw hammers the window-pane.

From Mount Tamalpais

The brown-winged hawks
Hover and glide
Below the rock
While from its shade

I watch them crest
Over ridge and hill;
They seem at rest,
Not flight, for all

Their effort lies
In sensed surrender
To the heat's rise
From the earth under

In which suspense
Their cruise would appear
Less hunt than dance
With shadow and air.

Thoughts While Travelling at Night
translated from the Chinese of Du Fu

Light breeze on the fine grass.
I stand alone at the mast.

Stars lean on the vast wild plain.
Moon bobs in the Great River's spate.

Letters have brought no fame.
Office? Too old to obtain.

Drifting, what am I like?
A gull between earth and sky.

Aubade

Wake up! The smudge of dawn
Low on the hills has shot
The bay with light. Don't miss
These minutes. This is not

Pure altruism, though.
I grant I want to see
Your face against the dawn.
Wake up, therefore, for me.

The Yellow Cricket

The cricket, vivid
Wings closed fast
In caution, sits
Unnoticed. Trust

Or extreme fear
Sets him to flight,
Charging the grey
Splinter with bright

Gold flame, unthought of,
Now revealed—
Like love that has
Lain long concealed.

You will one day
Find charged in me
What wariness
Disguises. See

How he now squats,
As drab as dust.
Love, let it not
Be fear but trust.

The Sultan's Turret

Dawnlight; I wake; and wait for you, uneasy
With early dreams: r.e.m., twist and mutter—
Here, let me touch your shoulder. Hmm. Real.
Rub eyes. The room asserts itself, a clutter
Of books—my jeans, your jeans (← fertile; sleazy →)
An upset yoghurt dripping through my socks.
Dawnlight: striations on the ceiling now.
Aurora—and her sister Mocha too?
But I'm content, wombed in the quilt with you,
To let the car-hums, chirrups, ticks and tocks
And your soft breathing hold me till I feel
Far sleepier—and awaker too, somehow,
Than I . . . the light sheathes your reluctant head,
You blink, I smile. We kiss. 'Your turn.' I nod.
(Duty, Stern Daughter of the Voice of God!)
The errant Coffeeman gets out of bed.

At Evening

Let me not sleep, let me not think, let me
Not ache with inconsistent tenderness.
It was untenable delight; we're free—
Separate, equal—and if loverless,
Love consumes time which is more dear than love,
More unreplicable. With everything
Thus posited, the choice was clear enough
And daylight ratified our reckoning.

Now only movement marks the birds from the pines;
Now it is dark; the blinded stars appear;
I am alone; you cannot read these lines
Who are with me when no one else is here,
Who are with me and cannot hear my voice
And take my hand and abrogate the choice.

Moonless Night

Moonless night; no phosphorescence;
                no line of land or sea.
Fractured noise, randomly rising
                and falling endlessly.
Dark erratic recollection:
                the driftwood, pearls and slime;
Love; love's passing; dissipated
                ability and time.
Patternless delight and wreckage
                without restraint or norm.
Strange, though; even here perhaps one
                discerns ingenerate form:
Certainty; pause; the return to uncertainty
                as the breakers assaulting the sand
Gather slowly, loose their power,
                then ebb away from land.

Guest

I woke. He mumbled things in the next bed.
I lay there for an hour or so. At four
The alarm rang. He got out of bed. He wore
Nothing. I felt his sleepy classic head
And long-limbed body stir my quiescent heart.
I'd thought that I was free. Wrong from the start.
I found I loved him utterly instead.

There was no real hope. 'Guy loving guy?
Man—that's a weird trip—and not for me.'
I accepted that. But next day, warily,
We coiled to snap or spring. Rash truth. To lie
Still could have spared the trust; the warmth as well.
I left his room that day. I try to tell
Myself this sorrow like this ink will dry.

The Balcony

If I have bent so far and not snapped, it
cannot destroy me now. This thing will pass
as it has passed before. Elation is
no birthright. This room is the same. The grass

in post-drought green, the violet hills, this light
of early evening are the same. I stare
out from my balcony, like one who's lost
the threads of his obsessions, hardly aware

that from the darkening sky peace falls upon
my world, or on the car-park where, below,
two lovers ferry groceries from their car
and kiss. My eyes jaywalk the road and go

to where you live, jog, laugh, toke, talk—and I
am suddenly glad that I've survived this love
and that it too survives. Now there's no hope
it's strange that this should seem almost enough.

Even Such

I saw him turn
With worried haste
And the world's fear
From me. I shall

Through month and year
Stitch up the rags
And will unlearn
The evident way.

The pain-dense tracks
Dark in the mist
Will see snow fall.
I will retaste

The tang of day,
The ceased belief
That paths exist
Outside this grief.

Close of Play

We are the last generations. Surdas, Bach,
Rembrandt, Du Fu, all life, love, work and worth
Will end in the particular rain. Computers
And chisels will rust, unpeopled city by city,
Beijing and Boston, Rome, Madras, grow still.
The kolkhoz milkmaid, the Basque goatherd, the peasant
Eking his sustenance from the Nile's silt; old
And young; black, brown; the Rio millionaire
And those who starve in the favela; without
Discrimination, justice or injustice,
Antagonist and indifferent alike
Will house the charge of death, and as the dust
Dissolves in the sea, the dolphins too, the complex
Whales. Seaweed may still survive; life's sap
May permeate a crippled grass; but we,
'The roof and crown of things', if such we are,
Will be defunct.

A mote held up against bright clouds of stars
The earth will move through universal time
And humankind will not be missed. If some
Distant intelligence scans the earth some day,
Mozart will be vibrations to them. Our relics,

Our alien skeletons, and the history
That led us to the radiance we attained
Will make them merely curious; but to assign
Human feelings to beings with their own
Is fanciful; who knows what they will sense
When data of this planet and the signs
Of an extinct consciousness reach them, its marks
Of art, its dwellings, its Great Wall, its highways,
Its books in which decipherable lie
Passion and knowledge?

The six-year-old's giant snowball slips
Down to the valley. He runs after it
To the far slope, then falls, and it rolls back
Its accreted mass to crush him. Too late we perceive
Our playthings, grown autonomous, knowledge and use,
This practical, that ideal Good at last
Rear doomtoys that will undo nine-tenths of us
Leaving the breathing dead we call survivors
On a radiant waste. Viruses perhaps
May breed despite a thousand shocks. We will not
Once so mutated see a new live child.

The custom of frenzy, pride and fear will ebb
Only with us; soon fifty nations will cluck
Over their extirpative eggs: and governments
Will get their sages, journeymen and maniacs
As randomly as in past centuries.
The toxic madmen who come to sting mankind
Every so often will not forbear to appear
In deference to changed circumstance; and Hitler
Will not grow sweetly scrupulous when next

He froths in his bunker. Someone, sooner or later
Will view this world through the eyes of capable hate
And 'earth of the slumbering and liquid trees',
The apple-blossomed earth will nurse its dead
Or tortured and denatured crust, and our strain,
For all its promise, power and prayer, will die.

It is a pity. Life is, or can be, good.
To sing, eat, swim, work, sleep, make love—to be
Breathing and out of pain, to have the arm
Of one's friend around one, or one's ears surrounded
By the deep quilt of music, to see the stars,
To understand their fire—but here it grows
More hazardous—for what was it but that
That will now bring us death, this will to know—
And ultimate knowledge is not ultimate power
But ultimate and seeable helplessness;
And though it is for our few generations
To value living these particular days
Until the earth rejoins its fellow-planets
In common lifelessness, circling around
Their mother-star in deepening entropy,
Rejoin it will, and soon. It is a pity
But nothing new to an old universe.

Last Night

translated from the Urdu of Faiz Ahmed Faiz

Last night your faded memory came to me
As in the wilderness spring comes quietly,
As, slowly, in the desert, moves the breeze,
As, to a sick man, without cause, comes peace.

Party for the Retirement of the Oldest-Serving British Museum Reading Room Book Attendant

Yes, yes, thank you, thank you, yes, it has been
A very pleasant forty . . . fifty years.
Quite so, sir; how time does fly. I have seen
So many changes that the world appears
Peculiar now. But this place, not much change.
Well, yes, sir, that's correct, the lighting's new.
And now we're particular about checking; strange,
Recently, though, we have lost quite a few.
Marx? . . . Marx? . . . well, there *was* someone of that name;
Old gentleman he was. Sat at 10A,
Writing, writing, writing, always the same,
And foreign languages too, day after day,
Year after year. One day he left, and since then
No one has ever heard of him again.

Dubious

Some men like Jack
and some like Jill;
I'm glad I like
them both; but still

I wonder if
this freewheeling
really is an
enlightened thing—

or is its greater
scope a sign
of deviance from
some party line?

In the strict ranks
of Gay and Straight
what is my status?
Stray? or Great?

Bagatelles

1. *On the Ninth Cacophony of a Modern Composer*

First there's a fusillade of farts and thunder.
Then there is silence for an entire minute.
The instruments are finally torn asunder.
The audience cheers. There must be something in it.

2. *Rake's Progress*

'Cars, women, beer—there's nothing else in life.
This is the tripod of my youth,' said Swill.
Ten years—and now the tripod is the wife,
The television and the sleeping pill.

3. *In Praise of Urban Green*

When every park becomes a highwayed plain
Cemeteries and golf-courses will remain;
For every thinking man who is not red
Reveres the rich; and, next to them, the dead.

4. *Overheard at a Cocktail Party*

But empathy with the Id is the quintessential
Je-ne-sais-quoi—as it were—of the Existential . . .

5. *Mere Invocation*

O luminous, dark and serpent-haunted sea,
O ever-hooded, tragic-gestured sea,
O dolphin-torn, O gong-tormented sea,
And thou, thou unplumbed, salt, estranging sea,
O snotgreen sea, O scrotumtightening sea,
Incarnadined and multitudinous sea,
O finny-tribèd, much-describèd sea,
How weary of description must thou be.

The Tale of Melon City
after Idries Shah

In the city of which I sing
There was a just and placid King.

The King proclaimed an arch should be
Constructed, that triumphally

Would span the major thoroughfare
To edify spectators there.

The workmen went and built the thing.
They did so since he was the King.

The King rode down the thoroughfare
To edify spectators there.

Under the arch he lost his crown.
The arch was built too low. A frown

Appeared upon his placid face.
The King said, 'This is a disgrace.

The chief of builders will be hanged.'
The rope and gallows were arranged.

The chief of builders was led out.
He passed the King. He gave a shout,

'O King, it was the workmen's fault.'
'Oh!' said the King, and called a halt

To the proceedings. Being just
(And placider now) he said, 'I must

Have all the workmen hanged instead.'
The workmen looked surprised, and said,

'O King, you do not realize
The bricks were made of the wrong size.'

'Summon the masons!' said the King.
The masons stood there quivering.

'It was the architect . . .', they said,
The architect was summonèd.

'Well, architect,' said His Majesty.
'I do ordain that you shall be

Hanged.' Said the architect, 'O King,
You have forgotten one small thing.

You made certain amendments to
The plans when I showed them to *you*.'

The King heard this. The King saw red.
In fact he nearly lost his head; ~

But being a just and placid King
He said, 'This is a tricky thing.

I need some counsel. Bring to me
The wisest man in this country.'

The wisest man was found and brought,
Nay, carried, to the Royal Court.

He could not walk and could not see,
So old (and therefore wise) was he—

But in a quavering voice he said,
'The culprit must be punishèd.

Truly, the arch it was that banged
The crown off, and it must be hanged.'

To the scaffold the arch was led
When suddenly a Councillor said—

'How can we hang so shamefully
What touched your head, Your Majesty?'

'True,' mused the King. By now the crowd,
Restless, was muttering aloud.

The King perceived their mood and trembled
And said to all who were assembled—

'Let us postpone consideration
Of finer points like guilt. The nation

Wants a hanging. Hanged must be
Someone, and that immediately.'

The noose was set up somewhat high.
Each man was measured by and by.

But only one man was so tall
He fitted. One man. That was all.

He was the King. His Majesty
Was therefore hanged by Royal Decree.

'Thank Goodness we found someone,' said
The Ministers, 'for if instead

We had not, the unruly town
Might well have turned against the Crown.'

'Long live the King!' the Ministers said.
'Long live the King! The King is dead.'

They pondered the dilemma; then,
Being practical-minded men,

Sent out the heralds to proclaim
(In his [former] Majesty's name)

'The next to pass the City Gate
Will choose the ruler of our state,

As is our custom. This will be
Enforced with due ceremony.'

~

A man passed by the City Gate.
An idiot. The guards cried, 'Wait!

Who is to be the King? Decide!'
'A melon,' the idiot replied.

This was his standard answer to
All questions. (He liked melons.) 'You

Are now our King,' the Ministers said,
Crowning a melon. Then they led

(Carried) the Melon to the throne
And reverently set it down.

★

This happened years and years ago.
When now you ask the people, 'So—

Your King appears to be a melon.
How did this happen?', they say, 'Well, on

Account of customary choice.
If His Majesty rejoice

In being a melon, that's OK
With us, for who are we to say

What he should be as long as he
Leaves us in Peace and Liberty?'

The principles of laissez faire
Seem to be well-established there.

Six Octets

1

You have the slimmest body. The light fur
That covers it is lovely. Lovelier
Still is that gold-shot hair; that mouth, those eyes,
Smiling, unmetaphysical and wise.
Enough said. But beneath this you possess
That blend of gentle whim and forcefulness
That only a bartender of high class
Could have poured out. May I request a glass?

2

Hands held in friendship, hands caressed in love,
I watch you break a croissant, while above
The patio redwinged blackbirds swirl in flight.
O morning after! 'Triste' can't be right
—'post coitum omne animal'—it's suspicious,
Even this instant coffee tastes delicious.
It's drunk with pleasure and I'm drunk with bliss;
Sleep; Doonesbury; and sitting here like this.

3

You don't love me at all? O God. O shit.
You still 'respect me.' Thanks. I value it
About as much as one who's asked to use
A second hat when he's in need of shoes.
Since, I discover, my own self-respect
Is quite enough to keep my spine erect
Why is it true my ample self-affection
Will not suffice to buoy me in rejection?

4

So now, instead of Zen gardens, of why
Small Markets work, of loquats, of the sky,
Of kinship ties, of that house-shadowing tree
Propped up by iron poles, we talk only
Of us, only of us, and what went wrong.
Curious, I suppose, to note how our rich strong
Companionship has thinned to this lament.
Analysis is free when the rest is spent.

5

I've spoiled your mood. I'm sorry. Yes, I will
Keep clear of you. It will require more skill
To keep you clear of me, you who infuse
My music now, my sunsets. I could use
More fortitude and say the afterglow,
The coda too holds beauty, but I know
Too well that these diminishing chords of light
Will be resolved to soundlessness and night.

6

Here are the plums. Take all you can, my friend.
We will not meet alone again. The end,
Without, alas, a happily-ever-after,
Is here, but undisgraced by covering laughter.
If bitterness there is, still there was love.
What you and I have shared reminds me of
These plums that we will separately eat.
For all their sourness, they are wild and sweet.

Distressful Homonyms

Since for me now you have no warmth to spare
I sense I must adopt a sane and spare

Philosophy to ease a restless state
Fuelled by this uncaring. It will state

A very meagre truth: love, like the rest
Of our emotions, sometimes needs a rest.

Happiness, too, no doubt; and so, why even
Hope that 'the course of true love' could run even?

Progress Report

My need has frayed with time; you said it would.
It has; I can walk again across the flood
Of gold silk popples on the straw-gold hills
Under a deep Californian sky that expels
All truant clouds; watch squads of cattle graze
By the radio-telescope; blue-battered jays
Flash raucous squawking by my swivelling head
While squirrels sine-wave past over the dead
Oak-leaves, and not miss you—although I may
Admit that near the telescope yesterday
By a small bushcovered gully I blundered on
Five golden fox-cubs playing in the sun
And wished you had been there to see them play;
But that I only mention by the way.

Point Reyes

Diagonal rain. Waves scud towards the sand,
Crestfroth blown backwards. Through the clouds a strand
Of light rifts down to a silvered zone of sea.
The buffeted gulls circle it uncertainly.

Sleep and Death
translated from the German of Heinrich Heine

How similar they are, these two
Beautiful young figures, though one is far
Paler, sterner than the other; one might
Almost say, far more distinguished than him
Who held me in his arms—how gentle was
His smile, how blessed his gaze. It might have been
The poppies wreathing his brow touched my brow too
And strangely fragrant drove all pain from my soul.
But such reprieve is brief. I will be cured
Only when he, the other brother, so
Serious and pale, lowers his torch. Sleep
Is good, Death better; of course the best would be
Never to have been born.

Mappings

Now that the windsurfers have gone, equipped
With wine, some loquats and my manuscript
I breathe the chilled gold of late afternoon
Along the lake-pier. The breeze ebbs. A tern
Pauses and plummets. Mallards manoeuvre through
The weedclogged creek. The hills slate into blue.
I stretch my towel out upon the pier
And read the bitter lines I once wrote here.

That was a younger self. I want to touch
His shoulder, make him smile, show him how each
Sorrow and failure that lacerates his heart
Can heal or numb itself: the limb-trapped hurt
Of love; the search for what remains when we
No longer animate the geography
Of cell and sense; the unassuageable urge
For ecstasy and knowledge; parting; age.

A mockingbird begins a sunset song
Patched from the passions of five birds. I'm wrong;
That was no younger counterpart but one
Of a live clutch of egos. As I scan

My mappings of these selves—despondent, witty,
Calm and uncalm, lost in self-doubt or pity . . .
The courtier, soldier, scholar—I check the pieces;
All are still here, the old familiar faces

In one-to-one correspondence: words and moods.
The light has lapsed. I strip and swim towards
A wooden raft. The cool enveloping lake
Merges with all I was and am. My wake,
The wine, my breathing, the recovering stars,
Venus, bright as a plane, Jupiter, Mars,
My pulse, my vagrant selves, my poetry,
Seem here to inhere in a seamless me.

Moths

The brightness stirs;
Two moths approach
The bulb; they sense
Its braising touch

Across the space
Their spiralling path
Must cross to brush
Its globe of death.

Fuddled with glare
Their wings succumb
To the taut shine;
As they draw home

No fear occurs;
There is instead
An eagerness
As they build speed.

Divali

Three years of neurotic
Guy Fawkes Days—I recall
That lonely hankering—
But I am home after all.

Home. These walls, this sky
Splintered with wakes of light,
These mud-lamps beaded round
The eaves, this festive night,

These streets, these voices . . . yet
The old insensate dread,
Abeyant as that love,
Once more shifts in my head.

Five? six? generations ago
Somewhere in the Punjab
My father's family, farmers,
Perhaps had a small shop

And two generations later
Could send a son to school
To gain the conqueror's
Authoritarian seal:

~

English! Six-armed god,
Key to a job, to power,
Snobbery, the good life,
This separateness, this fear.

English: beloved language
Of Jonson, Wordsworth's tongue—
These my 'meridian names'
Whose grooves I crawl along.

The Moghuls fought and ruled
And settled. Even while
They hungered for musk-melon,
Rose, peach, nightingale,

The land assumed their love.
At sixty they could not
Retire westwards. The British
Made us the Orient.

How could an Englishman say
About the divan-e-khas,
'If there is heaven on earth
It is this; it is this; it is this.'

Macaulay the prophet of learning
Chewed at his pen: one taste
Of Western wisdom 'surpasses
All the books of the East,'

~

And Kalidas, Shankaracharya,
Panini, Bhaskar, Kabir,
Surdas sank, and we welcomed
The reign of Shakespeare,

The undigested Hobbes,
The Mill who later ground
(Through talk of liberty)
The Raj out of the land . . .

O happy breed of Babus,
I march on with your purpose;
We will have railways, common law
And a good postal service—

And as I twist along
Those grooves from image to image,
Violet, elm-tree, swan,
Pork-pie, gable, scrimmage

And as we title our memoirs
'Roses in December'
Though we well know that here
Roses *grow* in December

And as we import songs
Composed in the US
For Vietnam (not even
Our local horrors grip us)

And as, over gin at the Club,
I note that egregious member
Strut just perceptibly more
When with a foreigner,

I know that the whole world
Means exile for our breed
Who are not home at home
And are abroad abroad,

Huddled in towns, while around:
'He died last week. My boys
Are starving. Daily we dig
The ground for sweet potatoes.'

'The landlord's hirelings broke
My husband's ribs—and I
Grow blind in the smoke of the hearth.'
'Who will take care of me

When I am old? No one
Is left.' So it goes on,
The cyclic shadow-play
Under the sinister sun;

That sun that, were there water,
Could bless the dispirited land,
Coaxing three crops a year
From this same yieldless ground. ~

Yet would these parched wraiths still
Starve in their ruins, while
'Silkworms around them grow
Into fat cocoons'? Sad soil,

This may as well be my home.
Because no other nation
Moves me thus? What of that?
Cause for congratulation?

This may as well be my home;
I am too used to the flavour
Of tenuous fixity;
I have been brought to savour

Its phases: the winter wheat—
The flowers of Har-ki-Doon—
The sal forests—the hills
Inflamed with rhododendron—

The first smell of the Rains
On the baked earth—the peaks
Snow-drowned in permanence—
The single mountain lakes.

What if my tongue is warped?
I need no words to gaze
At Ajanta, those flaked caves,
Or at the tomb of Mumtaz;

And when an alap of Marwa
Swims on slow flute-notes over
The neighbours' roofs at sunset,
Wordlessly like a lover

It holds me—till the strain
Of exile, here, or there,
Subverts the trance, the fear
Of fear found everywhere.

'But freedom?' the notes would sing . . .
Parole is enough. Tonight
Below the fire-crossed sky
Of the Festival of Light

Give your soul leave to feel
What distilled peace it can;
In lieu of joy, at least
This lapsing anodyne.

'The world is a bridge. Pass over it,
Building no house upon it.'
Acceptance may come with time;
Rest, then, disquieted heart.

A Morning Walk

A web hung from the avocado tree;
The spider rested in the dew and sun
And looked about the grove contentedly
Awaiting visitors; and I was one:
Neither a Californian nor a fly,
And humming to myself in Bhairavi.

Foreigner, hence! he may have thought, but chose
Instead to squat immobile as I came
Further into his district. Did I pose
An unpredictability? The same
Was true of him—bloated, yellow, with some
Sepia blotches not like those at home.

Our spiders are much blacker and much thinner,
Patrol their webs with greater frequency
And seem perpetually anxious about dinner;
Thin . . . spindly . . . starved—Nirala suddenly
Came to me—Shyambazaar, Chowringhee, Strand—
His 'Bhikshuk' poem—all blurred in this new land. ~

My very turn of phrase—Foreigner, hence!—
Betrayed the web of jocularity
I had spun round me here; nor could I sense
The pain I felt at home where I could see
The hunger, half resigned, half desperate
Of those like me but for a freak of fate.

To wander through the streets of Calcutta is
To force the whole world's misery on the heart—
Children on broken stumps, staring with eyes
White and opaque, begging with hardened art.
Far from those eyes, blind in my stead, I wander
Among these affluent trees, and stop and ponder

How fine it is to share the world and not
Its need when there are those who weep for food.
Their children's limbs will atrophy, brains rot
Swollen for lack of it, while 'all things good',
Food, shelter, health, are mine; interests; loves;
The time to walk through avocado groves.

Living abroad, I have lost sight of home.
Locked in my web I have grown happily blind
And blindly happy, and few images come
To jar the fine strands of my peace of mind.
A clod is washed away; the world is less;
But why disturb my quest for happiness?

For me there is this bitter questioning.
For others life is bitter through and through.
It may be short but it is everything.

No Compassionate Being leans down to view
And balance things; there is no justice after
For those deprived this life of food or laughter.

I draw my easy non-consumptive breath,
Think life sweet, spin rhymes, eat my daily fly
And neither shrink before nor welcome death
But others, even those who fear to die,
Suffer with quietude, with spent relief
The final amnesty from want and grief.

Stump

translated from the Hindi of Suryakant Tripathi 'Nirala'

It is a stump now,
Its art gone,
Its ornaments all gone.

It does not stir with Spring
Nor bend like a bow when green
Nor from its flowers fly Kamadeva's arrows
Nor in its shade are sighs of travellers heard
Or tears of lovers seen.

Only one old bird
Sits remembering something.

ALSO FROM SPEAKING TIGER

The Humble Administrator's Garden

Vikram Seth

In his second collection of poems, Vikram Seth reflects on three cultures he knows well: India, California and China. He writes about Chinese noblemen and hermits; lovers whom he has outgrown or who have outgrown him; the night sounds and sights on a deserted California beach; the power of moonlight and music to both hurt and heal.

Summing up the effect of this brilliant collection, the poet and critic Donald Davie wrote: '[These] poems should have an impact far beyond much noisier pieces; for when did we last see a volume in which the poet's eye is on what is objectively before him, rather than on the intricacies of his own sensibility?'